THE LITTLE BOOK OF
Inner Space

Your Guide to Finding Personal Peace

STA

D1585522

RIDER

LONDON · SYDNEY · AUCKLAND · JOHANNESBURG

For James Hall Hopkins

5 7 9 10 8 6
Copyright © Stafford Whiteaker 1998

First published in 1998 by Rider, an imprint of Ebury Press,
Random House, 20 Vauxhall Bridge Road, London SW1V 2SA

Random House Australia (Pty) Limited
20 Alfred Street, Milsons Point, Sydney,
New South Wales 2061, Australia

Random House New Zealand Limited
18 Poland Road, Glenfield,
Auckland 10, New Zealand

Random House South Africa (Pty) Limited
Endulini, 5A Jubilee Road, Parktown 2193, South Africa

Random House UK Limited Reg. No. 954009

Papers used by Rider are natural, recyclable products made from wood
grown in sustainable forests.

Printed in the UK

A CIP catalogue record for this book is available from the British Library

ISBN 0-7126-7050-5

INTRODUCTION

Our relationships and responsibilities are an enriching part of our lives but we also need space just to be ourselves. We all need a place to which we can withdraw when the going gets too rough and the demands are overwhelming. That space and place are within you. This is your inner space, the realm of your spirit. It is open twenty-four hours a day and you have exclusive rights to be there. This book is about retreating into that peaceful and powerful universe within yourself.

Inner space may be an invisible world but it can offer real peace and a true sense of the sacred. Healing is also there, because those with a spiritual dimension to their lives are more likely to be in a state of good emotional health. The goal of being yourself is not easy, for the world eats away at our lives and the majority of us simply want to run away from time to time.

This desire to get away from it all is a common feature of modern living. It is not surprising when you consider the impact of the way most of us live today on our bodies and emotions. Equally stressful is the extent to which we have altered the idea of personal relationships during this century. Our lives today are characterised by a need to negotiate close relationships that blur personal boundaries and require an ever increasing ability to cope. This makes our need for peace and spiritual nourishment very great.

People have always hungered for peace and inner well-being. But today these have become essential requirements if you want to maintain a healthy life and balanced relationships. The way to meet such needs has always been through development of your interior life, the place where your spirit dwells. It is right that we should want to spend time in this inner world which can renew and refresh our lives.

Take a journey inside yourself now. Start with your place in nature, which is your 'earth space'. Then, go into your inner world. Let the many aspects of your interior life unfold, from the sacred space to that mysterious one of dreaming. Learn how to retreat from too many demands and to trust the stillness you find within yourself. Become effective at making space in this life for who and what you are. In this way you may fill your life with hope, love and peace because you are truly yourself.

When you want to shout: 'Give me space!' When you feel squeezed, rattled, crowded and pressured, open this little book. Let it help you *take* the peace you need and deserve. Learn to live in this world but not to let the world live too much in you.

EARTH SPACE

Each of us has a unique place on this earth. We exist in our own earth space which nothing and nobody else occupies. But, at the same time, we are part of the whole planet. Our battles of daily life and the noise, discomfort and hostility of so much of modern living diminish our natural feelings of this connection to nature. Yet, our planet is heritage and mother. It nourishes our senses, feeds us, refreshes our minds and inspires our spirit. Many of us have longings to be in the countryside. We yearn for hill, sea, tree and flower. An awareness of your earth space, your place in nature, can help you to maintain a sense of harmony in the midst of the human-made discords you must face.

ASK NATURE

8

Ask the trees, rivers, mountains and stars if they have some message to offer. Ponder on what your heart is hearing. Use it to regain a sense of belonging to beauty and creation.

WELCOME CHANGE

Plants develop differently in different
climates. Animals can invent new ways
of behaving to take advantage of new
opportunities. So throw out old ways
that don't work for you. Take up
change by forming new habits.

CLEAN UP YOUR CLUTTER

10

How can you expect to get inner space if you live and work in a mess? Clean up and sort out the clutter in your surroundings and you will be more peaceful.

AUTHENTIC MOVEMENT

All nature has inherent movement.
Early morning coolness. The colours of
sunset. The moon rising. Clouds
passing. The dive of a swallow. Feel
the natural rhythm deep inside
yourself at this moment. Let it out into
your day.

GROW AT YOUR OWN PACE

All living creatures grow at their own
pace. Humans are no different. When
someone demands you rush or work
too hard, they are taking you over.
This stops you from being yourself.
Reclaim your space by acting as you
naturally feel.

GET EARTHED

Leave the dead foods in their tins and
packages. Connect directly to garden
earth for physical and spiritual
nourishment. Eat much that is raw
and fresh.

MEDITATING ON THE DUCKS

14

Think of a quiet lake, trees and, passing before your eyes, three little ducks. They swim, dive their heads, and move silently on. They are natural in their element. Your nature is peaceful too. Meditate on the lake, the trees, the ducks.

TWO TREES MEDITATION

One tree was thought good because
it bore delicious fruit. The second tree
only had beautiful leaves but these
gave people much pleasure. Some
things are practical, others are not but
bring happiness. What does your
life produce?

WATER

16

When you are tired and worn-out,

close your eyes and flood yourself

with stillness. This is the spiritual water

of renewal.

BLESS YOUR BODY

Serenity is as much part of you as
your sexuality. A hassled person is a
poor lover. Spend more time on being
serene. You will increase your lust and
become more desirable.

NOAH'S SECRET

You know that every animal is
different yet the same. They are true
to their kind and to themselves. As a
cat is a cat so you are human with all
that means in success and failure.
Imitate the animals. Accept yourself.

HOLD A LEAF

Pick a leaf from a tree. Hold it in your
hand and study it. Was it in the spring
or autumn of its life? How do you feel
about its shape and colour? What
season of life are you in? What is the
shape of your life?

BIRD SONG

20   Search out somewhere you can hear
the birds singing. A park. A common.
A city square. If you stop and listen
you will hear them. You too have a
song inside. Listen to it.

EARTH

Feeling disconnected from reality? Find a cat to pet, some grass to sit on, or bury your nose in some flowers. These will turn on your earth spirit and anchor you back to reality.

AWARENESS WALKING

22

Go walking to train your senses.
Observe colour, sounds, shapes and
textures. See with new eyes what was
formerly hidden. Awareness is the
mark of a tuned spirit.

DISCOVERY

The significance of climbing mountains
is not to reach the top. It is the

journey that matters. Sometimes it is
more satisfying to stop and explore
where you have reached. The same is
true of your ambitions.

CONTRASTS

Imagine forest glens deep with cool
shadows. Now imagine sunlight playing
on water. You have such darkness and
light within you. Both can be forces to
free your spirit.

SACRED SPACE

Sacred space exists not only within you. It can also be a physical place where you find sanctuary and are able to withdraw from a busy life into your inner world. We all need such a retreat that is our secret. Perhaps it is a corner in your home, a favourite garden spot, or a countryside view which you can make special. Here you can find refuge and a fresh angle on how your life is going. You can return again and again to this sacred space to find a sense of peace and inner reflection.

MAKING SACRED SPACE

Any quiet corner of your home will
do. Make it simple. Put a single candle
there. Take a few minutes to retreat
into this sacred space each day. Light
the candle. Close your eyes. Breathe
deeply. Relax. Enjoy the moment
of peace.

STOP THE RUSH

Get up ten minutes earlier every
working day. Use that ten minutes to
slow down by spending it in your
sacred space. Silently. Alone.

BE IMAGINATIVE

If you find that you can make no
sacred space in your home or at work,
choose a tree. Watch it change season
by season. Meditate on how it is unlike
any other tree, just as you are unique.
Count the branches as you count the
many aspects of yourself. The tree is
your sister. The place where you stand
is your sacred space.

BOUNDARIES ARE GOOD

Boundaries are good because they
give you and others space to be. If

someone crowds you, put more
physical space between yourself and
the other person. Then, close your
eyes and your mouth. Breathe deeply
into the heart of your being.

TRANSITION

Sometimes we need to go from one

place to another to change our mood.

It may be to the supermarket, the

shed at the bottom of the garden, or

just a drive in the car. If you need

this kind of space, take your little

journey now.

SANCTIFY YOUR
WORK PLACE

Make a place on your desk or nearby
that is sacred space. Put there a
flower, plant, or small thing you
treasure. From time to time meditate
on this object. Use it to retreat into
your inner space. Let this little ritual
remind you there is more to life
than work.

A HEALING RETREAT

A home can heal you: smoothing
colours, comfortable chairs, scented
flowers, plants, objects that you
treasure which remind you of good
times or loved ones. These are all
things that heal.

STOP SHOPPING

The world and his sister is out buying
up the earth. Do you need more
goods and more clutter? In your

interior life there is no space for
things, only the truth of your being. In
that inner space you will find beauty
and joy. Let yourself yearn for these
priceless possessions. Being more is
better than buying more.

WET BABY RETREAT

34 If you can find no peace or quiet, go
have a bath. Use the water, warmth
and luxury as sacred space. Become
your inner child. Return to a
mothering place of nurture and peace.

BEAUTY GIVES SPACE

That which is beautiful does not
threaten you. Bring beauty into
your life and you will find more space
to be yourself.

DECISION-MAKING SPACE

Garden sheds, garages, and bathrooms
are good places to think about a
problem, because you can be alone.
This helps you enter your inner space.
Here you can bring all your thoughts
together and measure them by
intuition and experience.

GARDEN WATCH

Pick a spot in a garden, maybe a
place you pass on the way to work.
Keep watch on it everyday. Note how
the plants grow, sometimes pretty,
sometimes sad. Change is in the
nature of all things. You are like
the plants.

VANISHING ACT

38

Vanish for the day by becoming someone else. Change the way you live from the time you get up until you go to bed. The clothes, the talk, the food, the people, the lot. You will reappear refreshed.

INNER SPACE

When we feel lost, confused, angry or hurt, we
need space to find out why. The answers lie
within us. Getting in touch with them gives us
freedom to recover our balance. When we are
overwhelmed with demands and the noise and
confusion of the world, we need peace. Such a
sanctuary is inside us. Going there gives us a
retreat from the world. This wonderful place of
healing and peace is our inner space.

LEARN TO BE STILL

Being still is not easy for contemporary
people. It needs practice. Sit down. Put
your body in a comfortable position.
You will probably fidget: move a hand,
cross your legs, re-arrange your body.
Do not worry, just relax. Try it for
three minutes. Next time try for five,
then ten minutes. Do this every
morning. Learning to be still is to
access your inner space.

40

YOU ARE UNIQUE

Take a hand-mirror, study your face.

Think these thoughts: *I am one of a kind. I am unique in this world. No one is quite like me.* Now, think them again. Believe them this time.

THINK PEACE

Imagine a peaceful scene. Recall a
moment of happiness. Hold peaceful
thoughts. Soon you will have
interior peace.

REFUSE THE WORLD

When you are overwhelmed with self-destructive thoughts or feel driven up the wall, give up all claims on the world around you. Have nothing to do with any of it. In a little while you will once again rest in your own inner space.

FAILING TO FIND SPACE

44

The capacity to tolerate failure is of crucial importance to gaining inner space. If you try and it does not happen, then relax. Let go of your struggle to succeed. Try gentle physical activity like opening wide your arms or going for a meditative walk.

INNER SPACE
MAINTENANCE

Like your body, the essential self
needs exercise. It needs to be used,
rather than boxed up by events and
people. Use your inner space
everyday. Make recollection and inner
calm a habit.

POLICING SPACE

You don't let anyone molest your
body, so why let them trample on
your soul? When people try to invade
your inner space and the privacy of
your sacred spirit with their emotions
and demands, learn to say: *this far and
no further.*

KEEPING WATCH

Tensions and anxieties in others is
contagious. Learn to recognize how
others are feeling and you will avoid
infecting your own emotions.

BECOME PERFECT

Good looks do not last because they are of the flesh. But your true self is ageless because the spirit is timeless. Why not give more time to your inner beauty?

ILLUSIONS

The greatest illusion is that we
think ourselves important. It is the
cause of most of the world's troubles.
Being true to yourself is better than
feeling important. Illusions vanish
when you know yourself.

MOTHERS

50

Only fools despise their mothers.
Make peace with your mother and
you have repaired one of the
cornerstones of life. On such
foundations you build inner peace.

SING A NEW SONG

Is what you have to say like piped
music? The same old boring lyrics?
Maybe that is why nobody, including
yourself, is listening to you. Try singing
a new song.

SHAPING UP

52

Contemplate your life. What is it
about? What emotional baggage are
you carrying? Where are you going?
Such questions and answers focus you.

BECOME AN ANGEL

You are not a machine racing down
life's speedway, hoping that one day
you will get to a rest stop. You are
not just about physical striving and
mental endeavour. Learn to be alone
and silent for twenty minutes each
day. Shut the door on the world. Let
go of the controls. Imagine you are an
angel with snowy wings and very
beautiful. Reclaim your spirit.

53

SPACE WORKOUT

Make the room dark. Sit comfortably.
Close your eyes. Keep perfectly
motionless. If you want to itch or
squirm, resist these until they are no
more. Let your legs grow heavy, then
your arms. Breathe gently. Imagine
your whole body as quiet and resting.
Let whatever comes to mind float
away. Just be.

GUILT

Do you need to seduce the world
into telling you that you are good?

You will never be convinced because
feeling guilty is deep inside yourself.
Only you can change that part of your
inner space.

POWER SPACE

Learn what other people are really saying. Only about eight per cent of our communication is words. The rest is in our body, our tone of voice, our movements. You can learn to read what others are communicating to you by observing these non-verbal activities. The stiller you are inside and the more at peace with yourself, the better you will be able to observe the true messages other people are sending you. This gives you more power to deal with people and situations. Your inner space is power space.

INTUITION IS A TOOL

Somewhere deep inside yourself is
that sixth sense we call intuition. The
better tuned your sense of inner
space, the louder will be the voice
of your intuition. Learn to trust this
inner wisdom.

Be content

Does a robin complain of the size of a worm? Does the grasshopper moan about the colour of his grass? Learn to be content with such things as you have. Your acceptance will bring contentment and interior quiet. Here is the power of happiness.

58

GIFT-WRAPPED
PERSUASION

A calm person confuses her
opponents. They do not know how to
read her. The next time you feel a
conflict arising at home or at work, sit
down, fold your hands and be very still
before you enter any discussion with
the other person. You are saying with
your body language that you are
composed, not tense or emotional.

Feel peace grow inside you. Now, wrap up your point of view in this peace and give it to the other person.

FINDING GROWN-UP SPACE

Even though you are thirty-something,
does your Dad always know best?
Does your mother let you grow up?
Tell yourself this truth: *I came into this*
world to fulfil my expectations not theirs.
Now, move them out of your inner
space. They have no right to be there.
Put them into your loving space which
means being yourself to those
you love. This will help relax those
familiar tensions.

BROTHER THUNDER

Thunder and too much protesting are
much alike. Both are noisy and usually
change nothing. It is much better to be
like a fine day, full of light and warmth.
Then everyone will be pleased and
you will be less exhausted.

FOLLOW THE STREAM

Instead of striving to solve a problem,
try an exercise in concentration first
to get focused. Close your eyes.
Visualise a gentle stream. Sunlight is
there. A tree overhangs silver waters.
A blue dragonfly darts by. Let the
stream float your problem into your
inner space. You have created the
moment to
find solutions.

SAY GOODBYE

How much of your past do you need
to carry? If it doesn't work for you,
then let it go. Be still, enter your inner
space, look again at what or who is
negative from your past. They diminish
your power to be yourself. Feel
yourself dropping this burden out of
your life. Goodbyes are good for you.

INSIDE OUT

When you feel serene in your inner
space, let the other person share this
place. Take her hand. Don't speak.
Look into her eyes with kindness.
Concentrate all your inner self on her.
Ask how she feels and listen carefully
with your heart. You are making
someone's life sacred.

THE LAST WORD

Let the other person have the last word. Do not be tempted to say it for that word will fill up your inner space with all sorts of bad emotions. Let your last word in an argument remain unspoken. Let it melt like a bit of chocolate in the sun. You are empowering yourself because you are letting anger die and inner stillness live.

LEARN TO TAKE TIME

The clock should not measure out
your life. Make time your servant, not
your master. There is nothing so
important in your life that it cannot
wait a little longer. The world and its
worries will still be there. Be late at
least once a week.

ZEN DECISION

We think people clever who know
what to do. Others we think stupid
because they only *think* they know
what to do. Now make that decision.

POWER TOOL

The tongue has the power of life and
death. Who are you hurting today?
Who are you bringing back to life?
Hard words never bring peace but
charitable ones revive every heart.

GIVE IN

70   Being stubborn takes a lot out of you.
      Knowing when to give in may be your
      greatest victory. It gives you a chance
      to use all that effort on something
      more important.

READ A DIFFERENT BOOK

If you always read romances or
meaningful stuff, try something
different. Too much of anything is not
good whether in books or life. It dulls
the spirit.

COUNT THE GOOD

72

Each day write down the best thing that happened to you. At the end of the week go back and read it. This is a record of your blessings. It will give you hope for the week to come.

TAKING THE STING OUT OF HURT

73

When people cause you pain, close your eyes, go into the interior self. Remind yourself that your life is special, unique and worthwhile. The essential you is not wounded.

JOYFULNESS

74

Joy is like new clothes – you feel good and other people think you're looking well. You can have a new wardrobe everyday because being joyful costs nothing.

PRIDE

If you are proud and fail, you have far
to fall. If you are modest and fail,
people will probably feel sorry for you.
So modest conduct is less likely to
damage your inner self.

HEART SPACE

Within you is the ability to live in a state of
loving but this does not mean you are someone's
doormat. Start by loving your true self, the real
you, not how you believe others want you to be.
By accepting your true self you will live in inner
harmony. Then you can become a force for love
because what you offer is real. Heart space is
strong space.

HOUSEKEEPING THE HEART

Keeping up appearances is okay for
your home but pretending good

manners when your heart is full of
hypocrisy is not. Clean up your heart
space so it shines with love.
It will brighten your day and the
life of others.

LOVE'S GOLD

78   How can anyone love you if they do
not know you? Mine your inner space
where the true gold of yourself is
hidden. Offer this to others so that
they may love the real you.

SHARING

Better to eat a bowl of soup with
people you love than to eat the finest
meal where there is hate.

SPACE PARTY

80

Close your eyes. It's party time in inner space. Who would you invite? What would you tell them from your heart? Act on these feelings so that those who you love may know how much you care.

THANKS A LOT

Go buy some flowers. Take them to
someone at work or home. Giving
helps peace to bloom.

LOVE IS KIND

82

How can you know kindness if you are always finding fault with yourself? Start being able to love more by loving yourself first. Just as you really are.

HEART WORK

A lover is like a gardener. Both have
to work to keep things blooming.
How is the garden of your heart? Give
it some attention today.

GET MARRIED AGAIN

When your rational mind – the one
that thinks too much – enters into
communion with your intuitive mind,
then you and your nature are married.
Use your inner space to think less, to
feel more, and to get balanced.

WHAT DOES YOUR HEART SAY?

85

What do you feel for the other person. Admiration? Gratitude? Affection? Passion? Look inside yourself and let how you really feel be the way you love. Your love will be true because it comes from within.

FAT LOVE

Your capacity for love should grow bigger all your life. Fatten it up by bringing how you feel from your head into your heart space. Here you can love people as they are with all their faults and failings. Generosity and understanding are the food of love.

INTIMACY

Sharing your deepest feelings is as
intimate as sharing your body. Treat
both as a gift from the heart and you
will be at peace with your decision.

BEE MEDITATION

Honey is sweet without being sugary,
strong without being overpowering,
full of energy and very popular. Are
you a bee that makes life a comb of
honey or a busy centipede that leaves
behind no pleasure for others?

TRUE LOVE

Believe that true love exists if not now, then sometime in the future. Your belief will give you hope and hope will open your heart to love.

JEALOUSY

There is no cure for jealousy. It is a
cancer of the heart. If you want peace,
throw out all envy. If you want love,
throw out all possessiveness.

MAKE ROOM FOR LOVE

If you base all your love on physical
closeness with other people, you will

soon find that moods take over the
relationship. Moments of silence and
solitude are essential for love to
flourish. Give inner space both to
yourself and the other person.

FAMILY TROUBLES

92

Everybody has family problems. If this
is so common why are you worried
about your own? Take your family in
your stride and you will keep your
inner peace.

In love with love

Being in love is only the beginning of a
relationship. If you are one of those
people who always needs to be in
love, ask yourself why you want to
remain a debutante of the heart.

SPRING CLEANING

Recall your unkind acts, harsh words,
and thoughtlessness. Believe that in the
future you will be more loving.
Confession cleans up your inner space,
but hope lights a flame in your soul.

SANCTUARY SPACE

How many people are you asked to be? Worker, parent, partner, carer? What about the basic you, the person underneath all those others? From time to time, we all need sanctuary from our role playing, relationships and responsibilities. Otherwise all the space inside is filled up and our sense of self and real worth is smothered. An always available sanctuary is within you. There are many ways to let go of your life in the world and retreat to this sanctuary. Practice will bring refreshment of the spirit.

RETREAT FROM
THE WORLD

96

Be silent in your sacred place. Open
yourself with the key of stillness.
Journey deeply into your inner space
which is endless and timeless. Let
peace fill you. You are on a retreat.

HIDE THE TELLY

Slumping in front of the television is
not a good way to find peace. Your
sub-conscious takes in the bad and
good, violent and pleasant. All this is
processed by your inner self. Cut
down all this emotional dumping into
your life. Hide the telly.

Smile back

98

Smiling faces make you happy and
good news makes you feel better.
Keep smiling and maybe good news
will come your way.

PURE CHANCE

You did not pick your family. The
sooner you discover there is no rule
that says you must like your sister or
brother, the more you will be at
peace with yourself.

DO NOT BE AFRAID

100

Fear is an occupying army, filling up
your inner space. Go on the offensive.
Seize control of your fears for all
problems pass. Soon peace will again
be the victor.

DISCOVERY TRIP

Why search in your work, home life
and relationships for the real you? It is
living safe and well deep inside you.
Book time now for getting acquainted.

HAPPY TIMES

The first step to being happy is to
know what makes you happy. Write a
list of these things. Make these your
goals because they reflect what makes
you feel positive. A positive self makes
for peace.

HANDS-ON RETREATING

Life can be too busy, too noisy, filling
up your head. Redress the balance in
your life through some small
meditative work of the hands. Some
embroidery. Polishing the car. The
gentle rhythm of silence and hands will
plug you into peace.

YOUR MOMENT

Close your eyes. Take a deep breathe,
rising your shoulders up as you do it.
Now exhale and sink your shoulders
down. Put your hands behind your
neck and stretch back your arms.
Finish with a big stretch and yawn.

LISTENING FOR GOD

When we pray, we talk to God but when we retreat to the silence within ourselves, we can listen. If your life is always filled with the business of the world, how will you hear God talking?

RIDING THE MEDITATION TRAIN

Meditation is concerned not with thinking but being. It is a ride from the known into the unknown. There are lots of ways to meditate. Try this one. Count one as you breathe in. Count two as you breathe out. Continue up to ten, then begin again. When your breathing is steady, let the counting go and travel into inner calm.

RUN AWAY

Leave home for a weekend
somewhere that is peaceful and quiet.

It could be a small hotel or a
monastery. The important thing is to
be alone and quiet. Make no demands
on yourself. By running away you can
refresh your spirit.

DEFINE YOURSELF

Your career, parenthood or
relationships may define the activities
of your life but that is not all of you.
You are many other things as well.
You have gifts, capacities, dreams and
hopes. Find out by spending time
within the sanctuary of your
inner space.

BE BRAVE

Are you rushing around being busy
because you are afraid if you stop you
will discover a lot of what you do is
unnecessary? If you are scared to face
the truths about your life, what chance
do you have for peace and happiness?

GOALS

110   If you set your goals too high you will
probably live a life of disappointments.
Expectations should be like a pair of
slippers. Accept what you can achieve
and a comfortable life will be yours.

CORE VALUES

Are you making up a personal culture
as you go along in life? This is tyranny
of your spirit because you can never
be sure who you are. Freedom is
having core values and living by
them. This gives the peace of
self confidence.

KEEPING THE
RIGHT COMPANY

 112

Foolish people have nothing to teach
you. They will litter your inner space
with idle gossip and ignorance.
Surround yourself with the wise
and the loving. These are the
bringers of peace.

CLEAR OUT YOUR HEAD

Distractions are like birds in the air.
You can not prevent them flying
around you but you can stop them
nesting in your hair. Concentrate on
what is important in your life and you
will have peace.

113

DREAM SPACE

Dreaming is always a vision quest because it
takes us beyond our rational world. It explores
our unconscious and proposes aspects of
ourselves that are hidden during our waking
hours. Do not dismiss your day-dreams as a sign
of laziness for they too are part of this vision
quest. In the dream space of your interior life you
can discover, create and act out new aspects of
self that bring insight into your life and
motivations. Your every dream, sleeping or
waking, adds to the vision of your true self.

SKY RETREAT

Find somewhere outside to lie down.
Drift with the clouds above your head.

Tuck yourself into a day bed with the
blue quilt of sky. Soon lazy dreams will
comfort you. You are on retreat from
the world.

FIND THE CHILD

Close your eyes. Invite yourself to day-
dream. Think of what you might like to
see. The seasons of the year. Your
favourite face. A soft and cuddly pet
or toy. Can you see a path through
a wood? Follow it. Rediscover the
inner child.

BECOME A BUDDHA

Finding the buddha within yourself
means you have seen through all
illusions and have gone from a vision
of things that pass to things that
endure. Meditate on the enduring
qualities in your life.

BE AN EXPLORER

118 When you follow a path, you follow someone else's way. If you don't know where you are going, dream about a new path. Let your inner space take you there. Find your own way.

SOLITUDE

119

Being alone is not the same as being
lonely. Learn to enjoy your own
company and you have made a faithful
companion for life.

LEARN HOW TO SLEEP

120

Restless sleep usually means you are
too stressed, too filled up with being
busy. Darken your bedroom. Shut out
noise. Make a place to dream in.

JOURNEY INWARD

Youth strives to engage with life. Later,
you need to find some wisdom from
all those experiences of living.
Disengage from some of the tasks you
set yourself so there is time to reflect
on your memories.

Everyone has gifts. Maybe you can't

122 paint pictures or make things but you

can still be an artist. Take up your life

like clay. Feel it. Give it edges, lightness,

colour, shape and vision. Surf the

interior waves to find your own

creativity. Be an artist of life.

BREATHING GOD

Concentrate on your breathing.
Become aware of it. This will help you
go into your inner space. Air filling
your lungs. Air going out again. Let the
breath that goes out carry away
selfishness and anger. Inhale
thanksgiving and forgiveness. Let it
renew and fortify you.

CLOUD WATCHING

You watch the TV and films. This stirs
you up. Try watching the clouds. This
makes you calm.

BALANCING ACT

We are busy filling ourselves up with

activities, goals and responsibilities.

Emptying yourself is just as important.

It gives space for making new ways to

live your life.

BECOMING PLATO

Those who deny they believe in anything often feel empty inside. Ask yourself what you really believe. Do not be afraid later to change your mind. The best philosophers were always doing it.

DANCE OF THE SPIRIT

Exercising can lift your depression.
Dancing around the room will free
your soul.

THE NEW YOU

128

Reflection can bring wisdom. Take out some old clothes you don't wear anymore. Hold them. Remember how you were when you bought them. Now, throw or give them away. There is a new you.

SHAMAN SPACE

Shaman space is the realm of experience or reality that exists outside the narrow, limited state of your normal waking consciousness. Here live all the spirits of yourself, all the primordial nature and the archetypes of myths that anchor you in your humanity. This is a place of truth and terror, fantasy and fable, ghosts and ancient histories. It runs with the waters of spiritual liberation. It is the burning space of visions.

STAR TRAVEL

130

Go out of this world for five minutes.
Be still. Let your mind empty. Feel at
one with yourself. Become starlight.
This journey is the most important
of your day.

CONFRONTATION

Do you have disowned parts? The
dark forces of your personality that
you unconsciously hide? Stop resisting
disclosure. Bring them to the surface
and know them for what they are.
Become emotionally whole.

THE THIRD EYE

The little boy asked the sculptor: *How did you know that there was a lion in the marble?* Are you missing something when you look at people and objects? Could there be courage there, hope, charity, love, or need? Cultivate your inner vision.

LIGHT ON DARKNESS

Guilty feelings are inner burdens,
hiding in the dark corners of yourself. 133
No one is nice all the time, so admit
you feel awful about something you
did or said. Better yet, tell someone
how you feel. You have shone light on
your darkness.

TURN ON ETERNITY

134

Really taste what you eat. Massage and feel your hands and feet. Listen to beautiful music. Smell a flower. Look at colours of sunset. Your senses are gifts of magic and echo the soul.

FESTIVALS OF THE SPIRIT

Rituals mark changes and passages in our life. Birthdays, family dinners, regular visits to people we love, church going, anniversaries, all serve to connect us with traditions. Make a weekly festival for your spiritual life. A special time, a special place, a special ritual to be yourself.

ONENESS

136

The spirit and the flesh do not have to
be at war. Both are part of you.
Make peace between them and you
become whole.

INVISIBLE BEING

There is nothing in life of which you
are not a part. Become conscious of
the unseen depths that surround you.
The voice of wolves, wind and waves
will help. Hear them. They are all in
you. Make visible within you that
which cannot be seen with the eye.

SING OUT YOUR HOLINESS

Use your voice to let out your inner
self. Open your mouth wide and sing
out all the words that pop into your
head. Never mind what you are saying.
The sense is in the sounds. As you
sing, chant or even sigh aloud, you
will release yourself into the
freedom of spirit.

SISTER WIND

Next time a strong wind blows, go
out and welcome it. Stretch out your
arms, close your eyes and ride it
through forests, over plains, through
city streets and fields of grass.
You are travelling with a spirit of
the imagination.

FIRE

If you are angry or frustrated, do not run away from these feelings. Turn on the flame of your true self and burn away these obstacles to peace.

VISIONS

Let your imagination take wing. Find
your secret desires. Watch them
dance, grow, become amusing, scary,
passionate. Now, put them away. You
have been on a magic adventure.

SACRED ROLE

We are all shamans because we cannot live separated from our own spirituality. This means you have a sacred role - you are high priestess of yourself. So act accordingly.

DARK SPIRITS

Evil rightly inspires fear. It is a
whirlwind that can darken your world.
All things pass so, like the Buddha, go
inside yourself where all is calm and
fear not.

FEMALE AND MALE

As light has dark, the sun the moon, and stars the sky, so you are both male and female. Do not despise the other side of your nature. Your spirit has no gender.

SOUL SPACE

The deepest self is where you are united with the eternal. This is timeless space without beginning or ending. You have reach the soul space of yourself. It is the place where love, sorrow, charity and prayer live. Here is where we suspend our disbelief and fill with wonder like an innocent child. We can no more disown this sense of holy presence than we can the stars in the heavens. It is the hallmark of our humanity.

GUT-CENTRED PRAYER

Offer up your thoughts and needs from the middle of your body. Forget your mind, let these things start in your belly and well up throughout your being. Many people speak more truth from gut feelings than from a brilliant mind.

STATE OF GRACE

No matter what you believe, be
comfortable with the mystery of the
sacred. Accept the unknown as a
blessing in your life. Be at peace in
your own calling.

SOUL CARE

Do you care more for your finger nails
than your soul? The most desirable of
hands will not get you happiness. Give
up following the latest fashion, start
appearing how you feel. This reflects
your real self. Better short nails and a
happy soul than a perfect body
and misery.

GOOD MEDICINE

If a person you loved was feeling
down, you would help them. Is your
spirit flagging? Does it need some
attention? Give it the tonic of silence
and sanctuary.

SILENCE IS GOLDEN

150 Nobody can tame their tongue. It is
like a little flame that can burn down a
forest. So trying shutting your mouth.
In that silence you may hear the voice
of your hidden self.

LONG LIFE

We plead for secrets of long life, but
our time on earth is unknown. Don't
run away from this fact. Instead live
today as fully as possible and as if it
were your last.

GREAT DECEPTIONS

Why are you so busy? Too many activities are a bundle of deceptions because we confuse being busy with personal fulfilment. Make a list of all you do. Continue the ones that bring you real satisfaction. This brings peace.

SPIRITUAL ADVICE

One monk said to the other:
'If you cannot pray, Brother, then have
some fun. It is better to make God
laugh than to bore him with
meaningless words'.

THE LAW OF RETURNS

154 Whatever your choices, something will
come home to roost. Generate
happiness and peace from within and
these will return home to you like
graceful doves.

SOUL GARDENING

A successful garden brings joy. It is the result of organising nature to produce the desired results. Is your life a garden or a weed-patch?

KID BREAK

Mothers and children both need time apart. Try putting the kids in one room and yourself in another. This is called *resting*. The rules are simple. No talking. No noise. No moving around. Kids can do it. Try for fifteen minutes.

WORDS

A person may talk of *concern*,
compassion or *caring* but be devoid of
emotional giving. Virtuous attitudes
without action do nothing for your
spiritual life. Giving yourself fortifies
your soul.

PRAYER

Use your feelings as prayer. If you are
sad, anxious, bored, angry, happy or
whatever, speak with your inner voice
about them. They reflect your true self
and personal honesty is a good way to
begin any prayer.

KNOW YOURSELF

Knowledge of self is the ultimate
wisdom. The world around you
cannot tell you who and what you are.
Use your soul space to mirror your
being. Look into it and acknowledge
who you truly are.

159

ABOUT THE AUTHOR

Stafford Whiteaker, who was a member of a Christian monastic community, is the author of Europe's best selling book on spiritual retreats, *The Good Retreat Guide,* and regularly writes and broadcasts on this subject. He lives in a farming village in France.